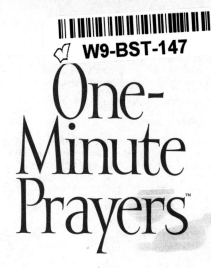

One-Minute Prayers™

FOR
Women

Text by Hope Lyda

HARVEST HOUSE PUBLISHERS
EUGENE, OREGON

W9-BST-147

Cover by Garborg Design Works, Minneapolis, Minnesota

Cover photo © Getty Images

ONE-MINUTE PRAYERS is a series trademark of The Hawkins Children's LLC. Harvest House Publishers, Inc., is the exclusive licensee of the trademark ONE-MINUTE PRAYERS.

ONE-MINUTE PRAYERS™ FOR WOMEN
Copyright © 2004 by Harvest House Publishers
Eugene, Oregon 97402
www.harvesthousepublishers.com

ISBN 0-7369-1347-5

Printed in the United States of America

04 05 06 07 08 09 10 11 12 / BP-CF / 10 9 8 7 6 5 4

Contents

A Great Day

So if you faithfully obey the commands I am giving you today—to love the LORD your God and to serve him with all your heart and with all your soul—then I will send rain on your land in its season, both autumn and spring rains, so that you may gather in your grain, new wine and oil.

DEUTERONOMY 11:13-14

∽

Have I thanked You for today yet, Lord? I meant to. Sometime between breakfast and my afternoon meeting I had planned to thank You. With each passing year I am beginning to understand the value of every clean slate of 24 hours. I regret all the years I did not understand what a privilege it is to be alive. It took me even longer to understand what a privilege it is to be me. You made me. You know me. You love me. When I wake up to these truths and let them sink in, I feel my spirit awaken.

I realize how lopsided I am from carrying past baggage. I bring it along for false security and sometimes to dredge up my list of mistakes. I am about ready to drop these bags at Your feet. In the meantime, I really wanted to thank You for today.

Renewal

Running on Low

*You were wearied by all your ways, but you would
not say, "It is hopeless." You found renewal of your
strength, and so you did not faint.*

ISAIAH 57:10

∽

I always dreamed of being a respected, productive
woman with many responsibilities. But my imaginings
shone the spotlight on a false picture of the calm, col-
lected, posed and poised, well-dressed version of
myself. But in reality, Lord, the tasks and commit-
ments involved in being a successful woman can
become tedious. I grow weary.

When I am running on low, I run to the Most
High. Lord, refresh my spirit today. Infuse my body
and soul with Your limitless strength and might.
When my legs are about to buckle from the weight of
real and perceived obligations, remind me to embrace
the plan You have for my life. I need to give You what
is on my plate every day. Only then will my steps be
strong enough to carry me on the right path.

Inside Out

*Create in me a pure heart, O God, and renew a
steadfast spirit within me.*

PSALM 51:10

∽

Forgive me, God. I give my heart away too easily
to things of the world. It is smudged from such insin-
cerity. It has cracks from moments of mishandling.
Cleanse my heart, Lord. I want it to be shiny enough
to reflect Your goodness. Mend the broken places, if You
will. I long to feel the beating of a whole heart once
again.

Renew a spirit of honesty and integrity in me,
Lord. I know how precious I am to You. Don't let me
waste that kind of love on trivial pursuits or quests
that end in heartbreak. My life is transformed when
this internal renewal takes place. Such a miracle can
happen only with Your power and grace.

Timeless Beauty

He saved us through the washing of rebirth and renewal by the Holy Spirit, whom he poured out on us generously through Jesus Christ our Savior, so that, having been justified by his grace, we might become heirs having the hope of eternal life.

TITUS 3:5-7

∽

Baptized in Your Spirit, Lord, I walk through my life as a new creation—a woman reborn into a life measured by her Creator's love. When I feel run-down or unable to move forward through the daily grind, I reflect on this spiritual act of rebirth and am instantly lifted above earthly concerns.

Women everywhere strive for perfection, timeless beauty, and a renewed physical package. Meanwhile they ignore inner flaws of doubt, worthlessness, and envy. May I never exchange Your hope for false securities. May I never trade the desire for spiritual perfection for the pursuit of physical improvement. My hope is placed in the only timeless beauty: eternal life.

Foot in Mouth

*Lord, I have heard of your fame; I stand in awe of
your deeds, O Lord. Renew them in our day, in our
time make them known.*

HABAKKUK 3:2

∽

"Show them, God!" Sometimes I scream this in my
mind when standing around people with hardened
hearts who do not understand the essence of life and
who work against goodness. I call out to You like You
are Superman. Save them. Save us. Save me.

You are all-powerful, Lord, so show them. Show
these people who do not know pure love and forgiveness what Your grace is all about. Change the hearts of
those who have bad intentions and who are self-
destructive. I have read biblical accounts of Your influ-
ential appearances. Why not renew such deeds now? I
want *my* peers, *my* culture to sense Your might.

This is when You return my command back to me,
and I am humbled. Hear my new prayer today, Lord:
"Help *me* show them You."

Plans

Making the Effort

Whatever your hand finds to do, do it with all your might, for in the grave, where you are going, there is neither working nor planning nor knowledge nor wisdom.

ECCLESIASTES 9:10

∽

This is my chance. I know this. I sometimes fixate on this fact. This is my one chance at life here on earth. You have given me this earthly body, this heart for You, and the plans You conceived for my life before it ever began. I pray that my efforts are worthy in Your sight, Lord. When I struggle and strain, let it be for a good cause. Let each and every effort I make be done with sincerity and honor.

Heaven's glory shimmers in the distance. I look toward it in my heart so I know the way home. But these days of living in full humanity also serve a divine purpose. I am to love You, love others, serve You, serve others, and discover who I am in the process.

Off Track

There is no wisdom, no insight, no plan that can succeed against the LORD.

PROVERBS 21:30

∽

I have a planner overflowing with...well, plans, of course. Each day's box lays claim to a portion of my life. I know that each time I set a commitment down in blue ink, I am also claiming a portion of the time You have planned for me. I imagine I am steering things in the wrong direction more times than not. I take great comfort in knowing You are able to guide my random efforts back to Your intention for my life.

As I make plans for the days ahead, may I seek Your guidance, Your priorities, and Your will. When I follow Your direction, the meaning of each day is magnified. The possibilities to serve You become clear.

Forever Heart

But the plans of the LORD stand firm forever, the purposes of his heart through all generations.

PSALM 33:11

∽

Lord, I spend most of my time pursuing goals and dreams that are temporal. Maybe that is the hardest part about being human—knowing that the future dreams I have might not come to fruition. There is an expiration date on my life and these dreams.

When I turn to Your plan for eternal life, I face a lasting hope. The purposes of Your heart have accompanied generations before me, and they will carry future generations heavenward. I hold tightly to Your promises and know they will live on when my other dreams have faded. It is a wonderful gift You give me...something to believe in...a dream come true.

The First Step

In his heart a man plans his course, but the LORD determines his steps.

PROVERBS 16:9

∽

I have great intentions, Lord. You know my heart carries with it many hopes and plans. Some have come to pass, and others I wait for with patience from You. But lately I sense my life shifting ever so slightly. One moment, my eyes are cast on a defined horizon, and in the next, they are peering at something hazy. Without my permission, without my foreknowledge, my true future emerges. You encourage my spirit to carry on.

Thank You, God, for letting me rest in the security of Your plans, not my own. Things change—sometimes so quickly that I lose my footing. But as I take the first step in a new direction, I know You are holding me upright and directing each step.

Grace

Overflowing

*From the fullness of his grace we have all received
one blessing after another.*

JOHN 1:16

∽

I have been filled with pride, overflowing with
love; consumed by longing, brimming with gratitude.
Want leaves me empty of satisfaction. Excess leaves
me bloated with regret. So why does my heart ride the
chaotic range of these two extremes when I have You?
Surely I have learned that nothing satisfies like the
fullness of Your grace.

For too long, my God, I have stepped over and on
blessings as I make my way to prayers for more blessings. Please show me all the riches in my life that come
directly from Your hand. Remove from my spirit any
longing, sin, preoccupation; the space they leave
behind is meant for Your fulfillment, grace, and will.
Empty me. Fill me.

Reality Check

For by the grace given me I say to every one of you: Do not think of yourself more highly than you ought, but rather think of yourself with sober judgment, in accordance with the measure of faith God has given you.

ROMANS 12:3

∞

Lord, I thank You for recent successes in my life. I have a sense of independence that is very fulfilling. But I know I am where I am because of Your grace. When I face moments of true satisfaction and bring my warm, fuzzy self-love into the light, I will realize how many cracks, stains, and faults this human vessel has. Reality checks are healthy. I want to turn my loving gaze back to You.

Lord, I am in awe of You. I pray that any step forward I make will be done with Your guidance. Your grace allows me the freedom to get caught up in myself. And Your grace allows me to return to You...dependent, thankful, and so full of love for my Savior.

Wherever I Go

The grace of the Lord Jesus Christ be with your spirit. Amen.

PHILIPPIANS 4:23

∽

Wherever I go, Your grace goes with me. I cannot be hidden from grace because it is within my spirit. You could have kept such a hold on Your gift, Lord, allotting it to those who are deserving on a daily basis. Instead, You fill our spirits with Your forgiveness and mercy. The world does not offer me security. I find it only in You.

I give You my actions today, Lord. I want to reflect Your gift of grace through my words and deeds. I pray for those people I encounter throughout the day... may they come to know Your love and mercy. May I develop a heart of compassion that does not hesitate to extend grace to others.

Place of Grace

Let your conversation be always full of grace, sea-
soned with salt, so that you may know how to
answer everyone.

COLOSSIANS 4:6

∽

Lord, I am often at a loss for words when talking to other people. In difficult situations of tension, grief, anger, or pain, I stumble through my thoughts and try to find something wise to hold on to...something worth sharing, something that is politically correct. I have forgotten to rely on the voice within that comes from You. As Your child, I can speak from a place of grace.

Lord, help me tap into Your love when I am searching for the "right" words. May I nourish other people's souls with a message from Your heart. And when I need encouragement, may I return to Your Word and immerse my mind and spirit in the language of grace.

Anticipation

But by Faith

But by faith we eagerly await through the Spirit the righteousness for which we hope.

GALATIANS 5:5

∽

Patience is not one of my strengths, Lord. It is a virtue I hope to develop as my faith grows and as I understand my life in Your will. It is my faith that enables me to wait at all. I impatiently wait for growth, an answer, a sign, a finger coming out of the heavens to point the way. Such a list!

Help me to rest in Your Spirit and in the faith I have placed in You, my Lord. I pray for true righteousness—the kind that comes from perseverance. When I am tested by trials and even doubt, may I be a woman of conviction and commitment. You not only see me through, but also carry me through these times. You turn my times of waiting into moments of moving forward.

Opening a Gift

So it is with you. Since you are eager to have spiritual gifts, try to excel in gifts that build up the church.

1 CORINTHIANS 14:12

∽

God, grant me spiritual gifts that serve Your body. In the past I have prayed for gifts that would help me succeed in different areas of my life. I wanted to give You glory, but I did not understand how the gifts I receive are meant to be given back to You and the family of believers.

The gifts You plant in my soul will emerge as I am ready to use them for good. May I never misinterpret Your blessings as permission to serve myself. While I anticipate the strengths You plan for my life, give me vision to recognize the spiritual gifts of other people so that I may encourage them and see You more clearly in the body of Christ.

Rushing to Do Good

Who is going to harm you if you are eager to do good?

1 PETER 3:13

∽

I can get ahead of myself when trying to do good.
I anticipate the rewards of the situation. I see how one
giving moment can turn a bad situation into a
blessing. There is the power to change lives and hearts
when I act on the impulse to serve You. Lord, direct
these urges to do good so that I serve Your higher purpose and not my own.

You smile upon a child who desires to please You,
who is eager to please her Father. Your love embraces
me and holds me close to the security of Your mercy.
How can I not be excited to share this comfort and holi-
ness with other people? I hope You are proud of Your
girl.

Waiting for Your Presence

I wait for you, O LORD; you will answer, O Lord my God.

PSALM 38:15

❦

My heart beats rapidly waiting for Your presence, Lord. I have called out to You in a moment of great need. I am so empty right now. I do not long for the conversation or advice of friends. I only want to be resting in Your hand. You know me so well. You see the places of my heart and my life that I hold back from the world, and You love me.

My lips form the name of my Savior because You are the sole Source of unconditional love. When I am emptied of energy and desire, I ask to be swept away to Your refuge. Just when I cannot be alone with my anxiety and humanity any longer, You answer my cries. Your mercy rushes over my worry and fills me with peace.

Friendship

A Friend's Prayer

My intercessor is my friend as my eyes pour out tears to God; on behalf of a man he pleads with God as a man pleads for his friend.

JOB 16:20-21

❧

My friend, who knows the Holy Spirit, prays for me, Lord. I am comforted by this knowledge. I can be tumbling headlong into a hectic day of work, and all of a sudden realize I have been bathed in prayer. I receive peace from the efforts of another.

My words to You come from my heart and are meaningful through the Spirit's interpretation. Yet, I find a deeper comfort knowing that a friend lifts up words to Your ears. She calls upon the Holy Spirit to hear her pleas on my behalf. I have a friend who knows Jesus, and we both have a friend in You. Thank You, Lord.

Friends in High Places

I am a friend to all who fear you, to all who follow your precepts.

PSALM 119:63

∽

There was a time when I followed the steps of those who did not care about Your existence. I emulated their mannerisms, which reflected worldly poise. I am thankful I woke up from this false dream. When I noticed You on the perimeter of life, I knew right away that I had set my sights too low for myself. There was something greater...no, Someone greater to follow.

I thank You for bringing godly people into my life. My path is not always straight. I wander. I take long detours that should be day trips. My friends who know You and fear You with their every breath give me directions back to Your way. They stay true to Your precepts; You stay true to me.

Misplaced Friendship

Anyone who chooses to be a friend of the world becomes an enemy of God.

JAMES 4:4

∽

Forgive me, Lord, for the times when I choose the world over You. With all You have done for me, I cannot believe I am still tempted by the world. Yet I am. I think it relates to my insecurities. The times when I do not trust You are the times when someone else's success or position in life has influence over my heart.

Recently, I have felt a need to be accepted by the world. Forgive me for leaning toward the artificial light of the world when I have the brilliance of Your glory in my heart. The trivial needs will pass, and I will be left with truth—Your truth. Lead me back to You, Lord. I do not want any part of me to flow against Your will…even my longings.

Making a Connection

*If one falls down, his friend can help him up. But pity
the man who falls and has no one to help him up!*

ECCLESIASTES 4:10

∽

I have a full life: family, work, church, commit-
ments. But I am missing the connection of a close
friend. I have had that in my life, so I understand what
is lacking. I turn to You with my concerns and my
joys, Lord, just as I should. But I need a friend of the
flesh, who experiences the trials of life as I do. You
know my heart intimately. Now I want to share it with
a special friend.

Please let me be open to whom this friend might
be. Perhaps it is someone already in my life. Maybe
You are directing a stranger to cross paths with me. Let
my judgment be put aside. I don't want to miss the
chance to connect with someone You have chosen for
me. I believe friendships lead us to a deeper relationship with You. I cannot wait to meet the special friend
You have for me.

Responsibility

The Greater Good

For it is God who works in you to will and to act according to his good purpose.

PHILIPPIANS 2:13

❧

The other day I felt You move within me. I was ready to denounce my responsibility. I was ready to distance myself from a commitment. And You prodded my soul to act wisely and in a godly way. I didn't fully understand it at the time, but I see now that You were leading me toward a higher purpose.

Just when I think all circumstances come down to what I want versus what other people want, You step in and remind me that there is indeed a good purpose to be fulfilled. I thank You for this new perspective. May I be aware of how the greater purpose affects the faith of those around me. Work in me. Work through me. Lord, use me as You wish.

Remaining

*Brothers, each man, as responsible to God, should
remain in the situation God called him to.*

1 CORINTHIANS 7:24

∽

I want to shed my current situation. But I know You
have called me to be here. This "now" I am experi-
encing is within Your will. I sense that when I pray for
release. You ask me to be patient, willing, and open.

I am overwhelmed by responsibilities I juggle in
life. Ordering their priority is not simple. Help me
realize that I don't have to understand how all these
pieces fit together in a master plan. My only responsibility is to You. My commitment to rest in my current
situation is an act of faith. I follow Your call and hold
onto the hope of things to come.

Working Toward Maturity

*Perseverance must finish its work so that you may
be mature and complete, not lacking anything.*

JAMES 1:4

&

That problem I neglected to give over to You has
circled back to me again. While I did not bring it to
You, I did toss it into the cosmos, and I thought it
would sort of drift forever. Well, it is here now for a
return engagement. Lord, help me give this to You
once and for all. Then give me strength to learn the
lesson of perseverance.

I require so much work, Lord, and yet You continue
to provide me with what I need, when I need it. I
never lack for anything. I am grateful for the times
when You called me to wait, to learn, to push through
a situation. You patiently work in my life so that I may
become complete in You.

Strength in Obedience

She sets about her work vigorously; her arms are strong for her tasks.

PROVERBS 31:17

∽

God, let me dive into the tasks I have before me at work and at home. I want to face my responsibilities with great strength and effort. I want to be hardworking in every setting. May my focus be to serve You, no matter what the job. When I honor You with the labor of my hands and mind, I know it strengthens me spiritually. Everything is connected to what is good and right.

Lead me to responsibilities that are of importance to You. Guide me away from fruitless efforts. I want my life to count. I want my work to please You.

Place

Creating an Altar

When they reached the place God had told him about, Abraham built an altar there and arranged the wood on it.

GENESIS 22:9

෴

Lord, I am ready to build a place of sacrifice for You. I believe my pursuit of many personal objectives has kept me from creating an altar for You in my life. How do I begin? What obstacles must first be torn down to make room? I have much debris to clear from my mind and heart, but I am ready for this to be done.

When the altar of faith is built, Lord, is my heart the only sacrifice I must offer? Your Son died on the cross and rose three days later so I would not have to build physical altars. Love replaced the law of such a process. Yet, You do call me to make my life a living sacrifice to You. I bring to You my every waking moment, I give You my dreams, and I give You my days. Please accept this offering.

God's Dwelling Place

I will put my dwelling place among you, and I will not abhor you. I will walk among you and be your God, and you will be my people.

LEVITICUS 26:11-12

∽

You are a God who does not reign from a mighty throne in a distant land. From the beginning, You wanted to be a God of relationship and love. You spoke to the leaders whom You formed from dust. You parted the seas. You moved the earth. You continue to work in mighty ways. As a believer, there is no denying how You have changed my life.

Even with all Your power, You still choose to dwell within the hearts of Your children. You guide by the Spirit, and Your love and strength are amazingly accessible. Create Your place in my heart, Lord. I want to be filled by Your presence and be counted among Your people.

Land of My Future

*Now Moses said to Hobab son of Reuel the Midianite,
Moses' father-in-law, "We are setting out for the
place about which the LORD said, 'I will give it to you.'
Come with us and we will treat you well, for the
LORD has promised good things to Israel."*

NUMBERS 10:29

Like a child staring at a wrapped birthday present,
I cannot wait to open the gift You have for me. You have
given me a place in the future, a place that is my
future. When troubles pull me away from hope, I look
to the land ahead and imagine the blessings You have
planted for my harvest.

I do not know how You will shape my later days,
but I do know I will never claim the goodness ahead
unless today involves a step forward in Your will. You
speak to my heart of promises yet to be fulfilled in my
life. I look ahead with expectation and belief. As I
move ahead, place to place, my love for You grows—
not because You give a gift, but because You remember
me.

Refuge

*You are my hiding place; you will protect me from
trouble and surround me with songs of deliverance.*

PSALM 32:7

∽

Faced with fear, I go inside myself. Emotionally I
curl up so small that any threatening trouble will over-
look me and continue on its way. I reach for other
people, Lord, but for true comfort and peace I prefer
Your presence. Your stillness inside my heart shames
away boisterous difficulties. Harm cannot come to me
here. You never said You would remove trials for Your
children. You offer something better: a place of rescue.

Save me, Lord, from the loneliness of this particular
struggle. Once my strength is restored, I will return to
the daily clatter. Right now, though, it does my soul good
to listen to the melodic voice of my Deliverer.

Longing

Longing for Company

And now, O Israel, what does the LORD your God ask of you but to fear the LORD your God, to walk in all his ways, to love him, to serve the LORD your God with all your heart and with all your soul, and to observe the LORD's commands and decrees that I am giving you today for your own good?

DEUTERONOMY 10:12-13

✍

When was the last time I spoke to You from my heart? Some days bring trials, others bring joy. Today brings a mixture of both. I am thankful to have entered into Your presence because I was longing for Your company without even knowing it.

Is my day going as You planned? Am I missing something wonderful, important, divine? Help me embrace today's complexities, questions, and ordinary demands. Somehow just sitting here in Your presence is changing my outlook for the rest of today. Did You need to remind me that You were walking beside me? My pace has been so fast, sometimes even reckless, that I forgot how steady a moment can be. With just a brush of Your Spirit, my day has taken on the color of hope.

Waiting to Talk

You will call and I will answer you; you will long for the creature your hands have made.

JOB 14:15

∾

I have allowed days and days to go by without talking to You, Lord. In fact, a whole season of life seems to have blurred by while I tapped my fingers and waited for change, peace, better things. Why in a time of drought do I forget to pray for rain? I have failed to keep up my end of the dialogue in the past, and You have been faithful. I suppose it is because You have not left. You wait. You move in and through my life and wait for me to respond.

So I call to You today, Lord. On my knees I bow before You and pray for You to hear me. Before Your presence covers me, I taste the dryness of desperate longing. I understand what it means to wait for a response from someone I love.

Savoring

A longing fulfilled is sweet to the soul, but fools detest turning from evil.

PROVERBS 13:19

∽

"Be careful what you wish for." Oh, the wise sayings of man! But it is true. The rush of claiming an object of longing pushes aside any thought of consequences. I know I set my sights on desires that are not of You. But the pursuit can be sweet nonetheless. Lord, help me see how these worldly prizes are empty.

Turn my eyes and spirit from the road leading to ruin. Set my path in the right direction. Give my heart a passion for Your knowledge, grace, and love. When earthly longings enter my field of vision, let me see them for what they are: distractions. Let nothing keep me from absolute fulfillment in You. Let me savor Your sweetness.

A Better Country

They were longing for a better country—a heavenly one. Therefore God is not ashamed to be called their God, for he has prepared a city for them.

HEBREWS 11:16

∽

My days have been crazy, God. I want to abandon my life right now and give it to You with instructions to fix it all. Some choices of mine have complicated matters. My inability to say no to requests for time and energy is now binding my feet and hands. I cannot move toward any greater purpose until I am freed.

So give me clarity today, Lord. Tell me which way to go, how to say no, when to say yes. As Your child I long for the days of heaven's glory and ease. Oh, how I hope there is ease. Meanwhile, I hold on to You and ask You to lead me through this life until I can come home.

Becoming

Purpose

The LORD will fulfill his purpose for me; your love,
O LORD, endures forever—do not abandon the
works of your hands.

PSALM 138:8

∽

Will I ever feel as though I have arrived? When I was a child I could not wait until adulthood. I thought all the mysteries of life would become known. And I was certain a sense of deliberate purpose would fill me. I am still not at this place of understanding, Lord. But I do know Your love.

Lord, work out Your will in me and through me. Make my days fruitful. Guide me in my choices and in my attitude as I become the person You created me to be. Let me carry on with purpose, trusting in Your love.

Stay or Go

In him we were also chosen, having been predestined according to the plan of him who works out everything in conformity with the purpose of his will, in order that we, who were the first to hope in Christ, might be for the praise of his glory.

EPHESIANS 1:11-12

⁊

As I question my current direction in life, Lord, I ask You to shine Your light on the way I am to go. If I am on track, I need to stop doubting my circumstances just because I am not fulfilled. I will not have an excuse to wallow in self-pity any longer. I promise to keep on the path You give me.

As a chosen child of Yours, I know You care about every step I take. My direction does matter. And my fulfillment directly relates to Your higher purpose for my life. Let me rest in Your love and Your proven faithfulness. If this direction is the right one, then I sing Your praises, Lord. Let me know, Lord: Do I stay or go?

Become Wise

*Take heed, you senseless ones among the people;
you fools, when will you become wise?*

PSALM 94:8

∽

Just when I am really confident in myself and my abilities, I realize that I get through my busy days relying mainly on wit, quick thinking, and sarcasm. At best, my skill involves strategic decision-making. But, Lord, I need Your wisdom. Life presents so many baffling changes and circumstances that my foolish, just-getting-by ways present me with little comfort and guidance.

Lead me in the ways of wisdom. I want to be Your pupil, Lord. I will turn to Your Word and will seek Your face as I strive to leave foolishness behind.

Transformed

And we eagerly await a Savior from there, the Lord Jesus Christ, who, by the power that enables him to bring everything under his control, will transform our lowly bodies so that they will be like his glorious body.

PHILIPPIANS 3:20-21

∞

Heaven is the place where we become complete. You will transform our lowly bodies into beautiful reflections of Your glory. Nothing will be as it is now. I am glad I do not know much about heaven, Lord. I believe that my earthly perspective would lessen the wonders of what You have prepared for Your children.

In Your presence, sickness becomes health, anger becomes joy, doubt becomes certainty, and fear becomes peace. I cannot wait to become one of the living...the eternal living.

Intuition

The Seeing Blind

*Like the blind we grope along the wall, feeling our
way like men without eyes.*

ISAIAH 59:10

∽

When I am not tapped into the Spirit, I let
demands, schedules, and requests direct my steps. I
grasp for anything that appears to be stable but am
often deceived. Help me reach out for You as I stumble
along.

Let me draw on the wisdom of Your Spirit. I want
to rely on Your truth to lead me forward. I do not want
to walk like a blind man, when I have been given Your
gift of sight through Your leading. May I be strong
enough to resist the pull of the world's demands and
walk straight and steady.

A Vessel for Truth

We have not received the spirit of the world but the Spirit who is from God, that we may understand what God has freely given us. This is what we speak, not in words taught us by human wisdom but in words taught by the Spirit, expressing spiritual truths in spiritual words.

1 CORINTHIANS 2:12-13

∽

Lord, give me the words to say to other people. Let me speak from the Spirit to encourage them, lead them, and direct them to faith. You give me the Spirit freely. May I draw upon this source of strength and peace at all times. My joys will brighten; my sorrows will lighten.

I praise You, my Creator and Redeemer, for You are worthy of praise. I long to become a vessel for Your spiritual truths. May these truths flow through me in words of wisdom. I rest in the peace growing stronger within me every day.

Tap Into the Gift

Let the word of Christ dwell in you richly as you teach and admonish one another with all wisdom, and as you sing psalms, hymns and spiritual songs with gratitude in your hearts to God.

COLOSSIANS 3:16

You are my hiding place, Lord. You also dwell within my spirit. When I live on the surface and ride the wave of materialism, I miss out on using the gift of Your inner teachings. I want my wisdom to be based on Your truth. I want to share with other people without a sense of personal importance. Use me, my Lord. Strip me of my self-dependence, and cause me to rely solely on You.

I have such gratitude in my heart because of Your goodness. I want my soul to be a place that welcomes grace and returns it to the world through kindness and compassion. Let my song of living ring with truth and resound within the hearts of other people.

Bad Influences

Do not be misled: "Bad company corrupts good character." Come back to your senses as you ought, and stop sinning; for there are some who are ignorant of God—I say this to your shame.

1 CORINTHIANS 15:33-34

❧

I should have trusted the still, small voice within today. I felt it even before I heard it. Then I coughed to drown out the sound, made a commotion to distract my spirit, and headed into the fray of a bad day—a bad day that just got worse. I participated in gossip; I let negativity override a sense of accomplishment; I pretended I was responsible for my own worth.

Lord, keep me from the bad influence of other people on my life. While it might continue, may I resist the urge to give myself over to false praise, pride, and words that tear down other people. My heart is better than that because it is Yours. I will honor You with a better effort tomorrow, Lord. I promise to let that inner voice speak to my life.

Charity

Lending a Hand

She opens her arms to the poor and extends her hands to the needy.

PROVERBS 31:20

∽

To whom should I give today? Whom can I help? Let me start the day with this question, Lord. If I am asking to be of service, then I cannot ignore the opportunities when they arise. I have looked into needy faces and kept walking. I think too much about such things. My mind asks, "How can I fix someone's life?"

You ask me to be a woman of charity and kindness. My actions to assist another child of God become a part of Your will for that person. You are not calling me to fix her, to make her whole. Only You can do that. My job is to lend a hand along the way.

The Riches of Hope

Command those who are rich in this present world not to be arrogant nor to put their hope in wealth, which is so uncertain, but to put their hope in God, who richly provides us with everything for our enjoyment. Command them to do good, to be rich in good deeds, and to be generous and willing to share.

1 TIMOTHY 6:17-18

&

You are my Provider, Lord. You gave me life, and You will create ways for me to follow in Your way. I should not question this, yet I have been in situations where financial uncertainty caused me to doubt the plans You have for me. I question what tomorrow might bring, rather than counting on what my Lord might bring.

I turn my circumstances over to You today. I will accept the goodness and the riches You allow. From the blessings You give, I will give to other people. I will strive to put my hope in You, God, not in my bank account. Let this step of faith encourage me to take bigger leaps tomorrow.

All Blessings Flow

You will be made rich in every way so that you can be generous on every occasion, and through us your generosity will result in thanksgiving to God.

2 CORINTHIANS 9:11

❧

The riches I can claim are Yours. They should flow through me and on to other people as You see fit. Lord, help me work through the urge to hold on to wealth. My fear of the future and my perceived need turn my willingness into reluctance. Keep me from blocking the blessings You have for other people.

Give me personal contact with those who need provision, or let me hear of a specific need I can help fill. My obedience can turn another person's cry for help into songs of thanksgiving.

Pure Refreshment

A generous man will prosper; he who refreshes others will himself be refreshed.

PROVERBS 11:25

෨

God, I have so much. Show me how to share the nonmonetary blessings I have: family, health, opportunity, stability, shelter, friends. Maybe I could invite someone to a family gathering during the holidays. I could encourage a friend with handwritten notes. I could use my health and participate in a fund-raiser walk. There are so many ways for me to extend Your provision to other people.

Refresh me, Lord. Fill me with the joy of giving. And let each offering refresh the spirit of another.

Peace

The Way of Peace

The way of peace they do not know; there is no justice in their paths. They have turned them into crooked roads; no one who walks in them will know peace.

ISAIAH 59:8

∽

Lord, correct my ways when I am walking a crooked road. I know the pain that consumes people on roads paved with regret, anger, or resentment. There is no peace along this path. When I turn my eyes to You, I move toward freedom. The chains that shackle me to past mistakes are removed only by Your power.

Present me with life lessons that redirect me and propel me forward in Your will. God, guide me back to Your grace. It is the way to peace. I know that in Your goodness You will honor this prayer, because that is the way of peace.

A Place of Peace

"The glory of this present house will be greater than the glory of the former house," says the LORD Almighty. "And in this place I will grant peace," declares the LORD Almighty.

HAGGAI 2:9

∽

This time in my life is not like any other time before. This place along my journey will be greater than any other because I know You better. I have held onto You through the difficulties and the delights. You have carried me from past times of trial into present times of peace.

While I have sought peace from other sources, I knew they were temporary solutions for eternal needs. That is never a match. But when I discovered You, I began a journey to a new place—a place of hope and promise that rests in Your embrace.

Affirmation

Yesterday Offers Faith for Today

O LORD, God of Israel, there is no God like you in heaven above or on earth below—you who keep your covenant of love with your servants who continue wholeheartedly in your way. You have kept your promise to your servant David my father; with your mouth you have promised and with your hand you have fulfilled it—as it is today.

1 KINGS 8:23-24

ꝏ

Lord, your faithfulness is so evident when I look at my life today. I still have my list of things I want to achieve or of the flaws I hope to turn over to You, but just look at how far I have come. When I look back on my past struggles, I see how You lifted me out of my trench of doubt. You told me I mattered because I was Your own. You also didn't let me settle, when settling seemed so acceptable. I just wanted a little bit of relief, and You were offering complete healing. How limited my perspective is!

Today affirms all that I know about You, because in the clarity of hindsight there is not a bit of doubt. May my today be a testimony to Your grace, which is so evident when I survey my yesterdays.

Power in the Message

But they did not believe the women, because their words seemed to them like nonsense.

LUKE 24:11

∽

When people question my message of Your grace, they call my words nonsense. They are ignoring the possibility of miracles in their own lives, and it saddens me. I can only imagine how it saddens Your heart. Sometimes my words are discarded before their meaning can be taken in...because I am a woman.

I am made in Your image. I carry in my heart a secret that is meant to be shared. Your love overcomes the deafness of ignorance, so I will continue to share the good news. And when my gender or my presentation of Your message causes it to be written off as nonsense, I will stand tall in Your confidence in me and keep on trying.

Resting in Confidence

*His master replied, "Well done, good and faithful
servant! You have been faithful with a few things; I
will put you in charge of many things. Come and
share your master's happiness!"*

MATTHEW 25:23

∽

I thank You for the many things on my plate right
now. I am able to help people. I work to create a good
home. I serve You and Your church with my gifts. You
are so faithful, Lord. You have affirmed me and my
current direction by blessing me with worthwhile
responsibilities and opportunities.

I am finding fulfillment, thanks to Your guidance.
I am more certain of myself, and my confidence in You
grows with each passing day. When I finish a busy day
and feel good, strong, and peaceful, I sense Your reas-
suring words: "Well done."

Just Ask and Believe

If you believe, you will receive whatever you ask for in prayer.

MATTHEW 21:22

∽

I believe. I do, Lord. And I have a whole list of things to ask for. Lately I have been slack in numerous areas. It is because I let insecurities take over my identity in You. What a shame that is! All I need to do is ask You for guidance, perseverance, wisdom, and peace for my circumstances. You affirm my faith when You answer such prayers.

In the days ahead I will look for greater confidence and security to replace my weaknesses. I will watch for evidence of Your power in my life. I have been here before and know of Your faithfulness. As Your promises unfold, the glory will be Yours.

Truth

Show Me

I have chosen the way of truth; I have set my heart on your laws.

PSALM 119:30

❧

I am so thankful I discovered truth when I did. I was all over the place seeking answers to random questions. I didn't even know what to ask in my quest for understanding and identity. You raised me out of my ignorance and showed me the light of Your heart. Everything clicked at that moment.

I still have times of confusion. I still have obstacles to overcome, but never without a measure of truth to guide me. Now my many questions are replaced by one request: Show me the way, Lord.

Absolutes

We know also that the Son of God has come and has given us understanding, so that we may know him who is true. And we are in him who is true—even in his Son Jesus Christ. He is the true God and eternal life.

1 JOHN 5:20

∽

Lord, do you see all the ways women are invited to falseness? A pretentious attitude and a modified appearance will get you far. That is what the world offers. No wonder so many women and young girls struggle with a sense of self. Your love grounds Your children in truth about their worth. We are all valuable because we are Yours.

Even if I cannot always tell which world image is real or retouched, I know the image of the cross is true. I can believe in You completely.

Words of Truth

Jesus answered, "I am the way and the truth and the life. No one comes to the Father except through me. If you really knew me, you would know my Father as well. From now on, you do know him and have seen him."

JOHN 14:6-7

∽

To be able to see You, Lord, is a blessing. Reading Your Word provides me with a picture of Your character, Your nature, Your love. While faith can be defined as belief in something unseen, my faith in You goes beyond that. I do see You. In the beauty of the earth, in the smile of a child, and in each victory of justice, I see Your face.

Each day I try to know Christ better. It is my way to move closer to the truth of creation and the truth of eternity. I am stronger than ever before because I follow this quest for a deeper understanding of You and Your Son.

Self-Deception

*If we claim to be without sin, we deceive ourselves
and the truth is not in us.*

1 JOHN 1:8

∾

To maintain my sense of status in the world, I
sometimes build myself up with half-truths. I have
moments when I would rather believe lies than seek Your
truth. I am weak in that way. But the bottom always falls
out from beneath plans based in deception. Sooner or
later I end up back at the foot of the cross.

I have such sin, Lord. When I compare my human
fickleness to Your godly steadfastness, I am ashamed.
But there is redemption in faith that is grounded in
Your goodness. I return to You and Your unchanging
truth.

Women

Sister Act

Now, O women, hear the word of the LORD; open your ears to the words of his mouth. Teach your daughters how to wail; teach one another a lament.

JEREMIAH 9:20

∾

Do I model Your love to other women, Lord? If I could be an example to anyone, I would want to show Your truth to women. Part of that truth relates to the ability to tap into one's emotions. Contemporary society requires such poise and control. We forget to teach young women how important it is to feel grief and pain fully. Difficult experiences bring us to Your feet. They reveal Your mercy.

We grow strong only through our opportunities to rely on You, Lord. My sense of ability comes only from You. I desire to share with other women the security I have found in my Savior. You are not only the epitome of love, but the definition of love. Your love for each of us is meant to be felt deeply.

Ask Father

*Jesus answered her, "If you knew the gift of God and
who it is that asks you for a drink, you would have
asked him and he would have given you living
water."*

JOHN 4:10

✑

It took me a long time to drink from the living
water. I felt Your presence before but chose to ignore
Your offer of salvation. I think of the many bright,
accomplished women who do not know You. On the
world's terms, they might seem to be filled with truth
and knowledge, but I know You have much more
planned for their lives.

God, I pray for women who do not yet call You by
name. I pray for the women who see a father figure as
someone who is abusive or critical or unloving. Let
them embrace the Father that I know so dearly and truly.
Show them the true, loving image of the Savior.

Keep Talking

The angel said to the women, "Do not be afraid, for I know that you are looking for Jesus, who was crucified. He is not here; he has risen, just as he said. Come and see the place where he lay. Then go quickly and tell his disciples: 'He has risen from the dead and is going ahead of you into Galilee. There you will see him.' Now I have told you."

MATTHEW 28:5-7

∽

You give me a wonderful message to share, Lord. You entrust me with a mighty word to speak to other people. My personal testimony is not elaborate, but it contains the miracle of spiritual rebirth.

You revealed Your resurrection to women, and Your angel directed them to share the news. I believe You continue to use women in this way. Your goodness is for every one of Your children. May I follow in the footsteps of those who loved You when You walked the earth. And may I continue to believe the wonder I have been shown: Your love.

You Call Me Daughter

Jesus turned and saw her. "Take heart, daughter," he said, "your faith has healed you." And the woman was healed from that moment.

MATTHEW 9:22

∽

Lord, I have shed tears over a particular hurt in my life. Though it is not a recent wound, it reopens when I am most fragile. Like many women, I let the daily stresses distract me from the pain, but eventually the heart and mind return to the source of anxiety. Forgive me, Father, for holding this sorrow within my soul, for thinking I could fix it on my own.

This wound never mended because I have never reached out in desperation to You. I wanted control over my hurts. I was ashamed to come to You. But today my faith leads me to You. I reach for the hem of Your robe and believe. And You heal Your daughter once and for all.

Relationships

A Worthy Friend

Likewise, teach the older women to be reverent in the way they live, not to be slanderers or addicted to much wine, but to teach what is good. Then they can train the younger women to love their husbands and children, to be self-controlled and pure, to be busy at home, to be kind, and to be subject to their husbands, so that no one will malign the word of God.

TITUS 2:3-5

∽

I thank You for the relationships I have with other women. Some have already walked through the experiences I am having. Their shared wisdom encourages me to keep going, to take a new look at my situation, to be thankful for the process of living. My kinship with younger women is also very fulfilling. I understand the role I can play as mentor, friend, confidante, and prayer partner.

Lord, in all my relationships with women, help me to be a good friend who reflects grace, not judgment; who offers support, not competition; who gives hope, not anxiety.

It Is Personal

For your Maker is your husband—the LORD Almighty is his name—the Holy One of Israel is your Redeemer; he is called the God of all the earth.

ISAIAH 54:5

✑

You are the love of my life. You are the Lord of my life. You care for and nourish my soul because You created it with all of its needs, intricacies, and mysteries. The times when other people let me down, or when I let myself down, You lifted me up on wings of Your faithfulness.

Some days I do not know myself well. I question my actions and my direction. My comfort is in You. You speak to the depths of my being and remind me that I am Yours, and that is all that matters. You are called the God of all the earth, and You have a personal relationship with me. Thank You, Lord.

Serving One Another

*However, each one of you also must love his wife as
he loves himself, and the wife must respect her husband.*

EPHESIANS 5:33

ॐ

Marriage is a precious gift. God, please watch over
my marriage relationship. Help me respect the dreams
and choices of my husband. Guide him to love and
cherish me as we work together toward our future. I
pray that we will always rely on You for guidance and
direction.

Let us follow Your example of unconditional love
as we care for one another. God, reveal to us the ways
we can serve one another as we also serve You.

Love One Another

Dear friends, let us love one another, for love comes from God.

1 JOHN 4:7

∾

My love comes with limits. I didn't learn that from You, Lord, so why does my heart restrict its capacity to love other people? When I am afraid of commitment, please give me peace to move forward. If I feel I do not have enough love to extend to another person, please urge me to trust Your command to love one another.

Love comes directly from You. Let me receive it with grace and give it with peace.

Freedom

Like No Other

I will walk about in freedom, for I have sought out your precepts.

PSALM 119:45

∽

Trusting Your precepts offers me freedom in so many ways. I approach situations with confidence because I know Your leading is true. I arrange my priorities according to Your will. And I lean on Your understanding when life presents questions and difficulties.

Your Word sheds light on uncertain times. I am so grateful to call You "Lord" because there is power in Your name. Your gift of salvation releases me from the bondage of my sin; thank You for this freedom like no other.

Never Go Back

It is for freedom that Christ has set us free. Stand firm,
then, and do not let yourselves be burdened again by
a yoke of slavery.

GALATIANS 5:1

∽

God, You knew what it would take for us to be free from sin. And You sacrificed Your son. There is no way to repay such an act of sacrifice. I must honor Your amazing love by standing firm in Your freedom. I will not go back to a life of slavery. I will not let temptation lead me against the way of grace.

God, I humbly fall to my knees and praise You today. Show me where I am resisting Your freedom. Do not let me take advantage of Your mercy by resting in sin. I want to be holy and pleasing.

Without Condemnation

Jesus straightened up and asked her, "Woman, where are they? Has no one condemned you?" "No one, sir," she said. "Then neither do I condemn you," Jesus declared. "Go now and leave your life of sin."

JOHN 8:10-11

∽

When I stand beside You, Lord, Your grace covers me. Stones cannot be thrown at me in my state of sin because You protect me. Salvation frees me from this condemnation. Even as a saved child of God, I return to a life of sin. Not as before, but I have fallen on my way to good things. Yet You raise me up to stand beside You. Together we face my sin, and You cleanse me.

Lord, when my shame is unbearable, Your presence frees me to walk once more in grace.

Use It Well

*Live as free men, but do not use your freedom as a
cover-up for evil; live as servants of God.*

1 PETER 2:16

∽

I have no excuse for my recent behavior, Lord.
Under the guise of Christianity, I have behaved badly.
I allowed grace in my life to become arrogance in my
heart. I passed judgment on another person and laid
claim to being right. My pride creates a mean spirit,
when a situation truly calls for Your loving spirit.

I ask You to squelch this stubborn way in me,
Lord. I do not serve You when my own objectives
become priority. I do not want to be imprisoned by my
sinful nature. Free me, Lord, to serve You well.

Speaking Up

Speak Up, Show Up

Speak up for those who cannot speak for themselves, for the rights of all who are destitute. Speak up and judge fairly; defend the rights of the poor and needy.

PROVERBS 31:8-9

⁜

Lord, I pray for the many people who struggle to make ends meet: the families who face a life of shelters and job-searching, the mothers who care for their children and sacrifice their own health and well-being. Lord, pour out Your mercy on Your children living in poverty and fear of the future.

Help me reach out to ease the burden of another person. Am I looking closely at those people within my very reach? Who needs assistance? When I have so much, let me multiply the blessings You give to me by extending them to other people. Your plan is not for a few to prosper. Allow me the willingness to be a steward of kindness and wealth. It is all about speaking up and showing up for Your children in need.

The Power of God's Voice

Can you raise your voice to the clouds and cover yourself with a flood of water? Do you send the lightning bolts on their way? Do they report to you, "Here we are"?

JOB 38:34-35

⚘

I can scream at tragedy, and it will not dissipate. I can shout at my wounds from past hurts, yet they will not heal. Lord, only when I call out to You, and You in turn speak to my life, can such things happen. My voice is meant to praise You; it is not meant to hold the power of God.

Lord, right now, my personal pain takes my breath away. I can only whisper to You. The words I lift up are praises. In the midst of my trial, praises bring me into Your presence. And there my soul is healed.

Wise Move

Does not wisdom call out? Does not understanding raise her voice?

PROVERBS 8:1

❧

I try to be a good leader, Lord. I seek Your assistance when faced with decisions, and I pray about my every step. Please let my words be filled with Your wisdom. It can be intimidating to lead other people when I do not have the right words and the right time.

When I turn to You before speaking out, You give me understanding. And wisdom calls out. I rely on You to be my voice. In my desire to lead, Lord, let my life be an expression of Your message of love.

Cry for Help

The righteous cry out, and the LORD hears them; he delivers them from all their troubles.

PSALM 34:17

∽

As I go about my day, I talk to You, Lord. You hear my every mumble. You pay attention to me even when I am ranting and raving. I ask for what I think I want. I insist that things change to suit my mood. Through it all, You still love me. You know I am finding my way.

Lord, forgive me when I bring You my troubles, yet neglect to say what is truly on my heart. Lord, I need You as desperately as I need air to breathe. Because You hear my cries, You turn lamentations into praises.

Holding On

Misplaced Trust

You have let go of the commands of God and are holding on to the traditions of men.

MARK 7:8

God, I want to resist the temptation to hold on to the ways of mankind. Early in my faith, I reached for and grasped Your teachings. I let them sink into my spirit and fill me with knowledge and light. Now as I ride the merry-go-round of life, I am tempted by the brass rings of easy solutions. I reach for them instead of Your precepts.

It is difficult to turn from old habits. I set my sights on those who appear successful in life and try to follow them. Help me release my grip on the world and its truth, Lord. Inspire me to hold on to Your commands with all my heart.

Reaching for Faith

Timothy, my son, I give you this instruction in keeping with the prophecies once made about you, so that by following them you may fight the good fight, holding on to faith and a good conscience.

1 TIMOTHY 1:18-19

❧

Lead me in Your instruction today, God. Let me clearly feel Your direction as I work and make choices. Maybe You will lead someone to speak words of truth into my life. I have received encouragement and wisdom through friends and even strangers in the past.

Do not let me feel alone in my efforts. Direct me toward the fellowship of other believers. Let them counsel me in Your way. I will hold on to my faith tightly today, Lord, and wait upon Your wisdom.

Letting Go of Nothing

Hold on to instruction, do not let it go; guard it well,
for it is your life.

PROVERBS 4:13

∽

When I filter out needless information from my gathering of knowledge, what remains are the eternal truths You provide. In my busyness, I acquire a lot of worthless detail about so many different things. I memorize addresses, pin codes, passwords, airport regulations, and word processing shortcuts. There is little room left for Your instruction.

Clear my mind, Lord. Details are important, but when I come to You in prayer, I want to let go of these bits of nothingness. Let them fade away so I can hold tightly to Your instruction as You speak it into my heart.

The Strength of Jesus

*But Christ is faithful as a son over God's house. And
we are his house, if we hold on to our courage and
the hope of which we boast.*

HEBREWS 3:6

∽

"I am weak but He is strong." Yes, Jesus loves me.
And I am so thankful. My weakness is more apparent
all the time. I should be old enough to know better...
about everything. But I don't. I take false steps in
strange directions. I strive to measure up to the world's
expectations. But what I really want is to measure up
as a child of God who needs the help of her Lord. I want
Your power in my life.

Help me turn my hope into true strength. I am
weak. But I know the One who lifts me above my circumstances. Let courage grow from my active faith.

Stepping Out

A Confident Life

For God did not give us a spirit of timidity, but a spirit of power, of love and of self-discipline.

2 TIMOTHY 1:7

❧

When I approach situations that make me nervous, I focus on Your Spirit of power that resides within me. My timid days are behind me because I have Your strength as my foundation. Lord, give me a boldness I have never known. Let me step out with security in You.

Life will be new and different as I make decisions, communicate, and walk forward with this power. I will practice self-discipline and express love through my actions so that You, Lord, may use this new confidence for good.

Certainty

*Act with courage, and may the LORD be with those
who do well.*

2 CHRONICLES 19:11

∽

Fill me with courage, Lord. The confidence I receive
from my worldly support is not strong. It wavers
according to my current level of influence or popu-
larity. It takes very little for my hopes to be dashed. I
long to feel certain of myself and my life. I don't want
opinions of other people to sway me from my known
path.

I will keep my eyes upon You, Lord. Your love is
my assurance. My faith and my salvation are certain.
The confidence I have in these matters will lead to my
success.

God Is with Me

Be strong and courageous, and do the work. Do not be afraid or discouraged, for the LORD God, my God, is with you.

1 CHRONICLES 28:20

∾

I think life is requiring too much work, Lord. I have tried all this time to be strong, but I am slipping backward. How can I keep up? Please help me continue through my trials when I don't have the energy to keep going. Break my stubborn spirit so I learn to lean upon Your strength.

I can do all things when I walk with You. I pray to be open to the work ahead. Let me not cower when You call on me to put forth great effort. It will not be unbearable. It will be the beginning of something miraculous.

Shine Forth

Commit your way to the LORD; trust in him and he will do this: He will make your righteousness shine like the dawn, the justice of your cause like the noonday sun.

PSALM 37:5-6

∾

Draw me to a life of commitment, Lord. Show me where I have sin that keeps me from embracing unconditional faith. I trust You with my eternity, so why is it difficult to turn over my here and now? Release me from fear and show me the life You have planned for me. I rise up and accept all that You are doing in my life.

Let my righteousness shine through even the darkest days. I will move forward as Your love warms me like the sun and prepares my heart for a great harvest.

Prayer

Praise

May my prayer be set before you like incense; may the lifting up of my hands be like the evening sacrifice.

PSALM 141:2

∽

I talk too much. My prayers don't leave room for breath and reflection. I petition without praise. Lord, lead me to a deeper prayer life. Even as I pray right now, I can let my mind wander to things that need to be done, or requests I want to make while I have Your attention.

Let me come to You in silence and with a spirit of worship. May my words wind their way to You like tendrils of burning incense. In Your presence I will surrender my own will.

Prayers of Protection

I have given them your word and the world has hated them, for they are not of the world any more than I am of the world. My prayer is not that you take them out of the world but that you protect them from the evil one.

JOHN 17:14-15

∾

I pray today as Your Son prayed for His followers. I ask for Your protection from evil while I am in the world. Being here creates opportunity for me to share my faith, to develop a deeper relationship with You, and to taste the richness of the life You have given me. But I know I am not truly of the world.

In troubled times I am tempted to ask You to remove my burdens or to release me from the pressure of life in the world. But You call me to walk in the plan You have for me. So protect me, Lord, for the rest of my days, so I can fulfill Your will.

Find Me Faithful

Be joyful in hope, patient in affliction, faithful in prayer. Share with God's people who are in need. Practice hospitality.

ROMANS 12:12-13

ॐ

May my life be a living prayer to You. When I cannot find the right words, let the beating of my heart do the speaking. May my actions toward other people be a prayer of hospitality and compassion. Lord, turn my fear into patience when I face hardship so I can demonstrate the power of prayer to other people.

Your Word reveals how to be a living prayer. I will glean from its endless wisdom and apply its truths to each situation. As long as there is need in my life and in the world, may You find me faithful in prayer and as a prayer.

Effective Prayer

And the prayer offered in faith will make the sick person well; the Lord will raise him up. If he has sinned, he will be forgiven. Therefore confess your sins to each other and pray for each other so that you may be healed. The prayer of a righteous man is powerful and effective.

JAMES 5:15-16

&

Lord, I come to You today with my burden of sins. I hold each transgression up for a second look at my humanity. I place them in Your light for a closer look at Your grace. The practice of asking for forgiveness is important to my relationship with You. First, I am humbled and emptied of self. Then I am cleansed and filled with Your mercy.

When I pray, Lord, I know You hear me. I become vulnerable in Your presence because I have great faith in Your protection. May You call me righteous, and may my prayers be deemed powerful and effective.

Health

Healthy Soul

*Dear friend, I pray that you may enjoy good health
and that all may go well with you, even as your soul
is getting along well.*

3 JOHN 2

✎

I have noticed how my efforts toward a healthy life
have also enriched my soul. I am clear-thinking, brighter,
more attentive to my spiritual needs. Lord, I know I
complain about this body of mine, but I ask You to bless
it with healing and wholeness. Where I am having
physical difficulties, direct me toward the right care.
Don't let me abuse my body just because I am tired of
its shortcomings.

When I focus on my breath and think about the
oxygen soaring through my system, I am so grateful for
the intricate workings of my body. I was made by You,
and I will treat Your creation with kindness—inside
and out.

Healing Toward Peace

Nevertheless, I will bring health and healing to it; I will heal my people and will let them enjoy abundant peace and security.

JEREMIAH 33:6

∽

You heal. There is no other resource in my life that offers healing. You mend my brokenness with Your offer of wholeness. You remove the hurts I have been carrying around for years. Not only do You offer healing, but the new life I am given is one of abundance and great wonders.

You do not call my personal fulfillment trivial. Instead You guide me in a way that promises this fulfillment. I thank You, God, for being so gracious and giving.

Unhealthy Living

Because of your wrath there is no health in my body; my bones have no soundness because of my sin.

PSALM 38:3

∽

My sin is like a wound. When left unattended, it becomes more painful, spreads, and deepens. The damage becomes more difficult to repair. But when I come to You right away, Lord, and confess my sin, the healing begins immediately. "Freedom from sin" is no longer just a phrase or bit of head knowledge. It is a real happening in my life. I actually have the sensation of a burden removed from my spirit.

Hear my prayers, Lord. Listen to my cries of repentance. Restore the strength of my flesh, bones, and soul.

Good to the Bone

A cheerful look brings joy to the heart, and good news gives health to the bones.

PROVERBS 15:30

✑

I need some good news about now, Lord. Recent days have been filled with sad news and frustrations. I haven't been able to focus and rarely get to bed on time. My spirit is restless. God, give me healing. From my flesh to my spirit, infuse my being with the power of Your good news.

I hold my faith close to me during this time. I take a walk outside and let nature's cheerfulness embrace me. Your presence is everywhere. You have not left me... even as I wait for good news and restoration.

Dancing

Recognizing the Time

There is a time for everything, and a season for every activity under heaven: ...a time to weep and a time to laugh, a time to mourn and a time to dance.

ECCLESIASTES 3:1,4

∽

You created a time for each season. You mastered a plan of cycles that allows endings and beginnings to flow together. Under heaven's gaze, I live through these seasons and try to adjust to them. Lord, I face a change right now and need to allow myself a chance to weep. As I face a transition, give me laughter so Your joy can touch my soul.

My time to mourn will be followed by chances to dance. I pray that Your presence will always be known in my life. May I never allow sadness to breed doubt when it is meant to breed hope for tomorrow.

Leaping for Joy

Then maidens will dance and be glad, young men and
old as well. I will turn their mourning into gladness;
I will give them comfort and joy instead of sorrow.

JEREMIAH 31:13

∽

God, thank You for releasing me from my painful experiences. The weight that pressed me down has been removed. Suddenly I want to dance. I want to leap with freedom. When I have seen the depths of mourning and Your hand still is able to pull me back to a place of peace, I have a new sense of what living is all about.

I bow to You and twirl across the days ahead. You are allowing me a second opportunity to feel deeply and to grow through sadness and blossom in shades of joy.

Sing unto the Lord

You turned my wailing into dancing; you removed my sackcloth and clothed me with joy, that my heart may sing to you and not be silent.

PSALM 30:11-12

∽

With all that You have going on, Lord, I am amazed that You still encourage my heart to express its emotions. One day I am asking for Your mercy. Another day I await Your blessing for an opportunity. You do not call me to be silent. While people rarely have time to hear the thoughts of another, You lovingly wait for my life song.

When my circumstances change, I owe it all to You. It is not of my doing that rain turns to sunshine. So it is not my doing when tears are dried by true joy. Thank You, Lord.

A New Dance

I will build you up again and you will be rebuilt, O Virgin Israel. Again you will take up your tambourines and go out to dance with the joyful.

JEREMIAH 31:4

∽

You are rebuilding me right now, Lord. I feel the growing pains. I see the unnecessary pieces of my life fall away. I watch as my new life emerges from the dust of construction. It is hard to be carved into a new being, Lord. Be gentle with me as You mold me into a creation that serves You even better.

There will be a day in the near future when I will dance. Music will flow through my life and give me a reason to shout with great happiness. God, please keep working on me. Your vision for my life is worth the wait.

Let It Be

Therefore do not worry about tomorrow, for tomorrow will worry about itself.

MATTHEW 6:34

∽

I want control over today and tomorrow. I know You can do a much better job, Lord, but I still battle for control. I don't have a great track record when I try to take the reins from Your hands. Let today affect my tomorrow. Give me the strength I need in this moment to give You my tomorrow.

There will be worries. There will be struggles. But tomorrow is also filled with possibility. I am inching closer to eternity, and this is a journey I want to savor, not suffer through. Give me the courage to live fully today and await tomorrow with great hope.

Books You Can Believe In
HARVEST HOUSE PUBLISHERS

One-Minute Prayers™

This collection of simple, heartfelt prayers and Scriptures is designed to serve the pace and needs of everyday life. Offering renewal, this prayer journey encourages readers to experience fellowship with God during busy times.

The Power of a Praying® Woman
Stormie Omartian

Stormie has led nearly two million women into deeper, more fulfilling prayer lives. In *The Power of a Praying® Woman,* through her knowledge of Scripture and candid examples of her own epiphanies in prayer, she shows you how to

- draw closer to God
- know His plans and purposes for your life
- receive comfort, help, and strength for every day

Trust Him moment by moment with the concerns of your heart and discover the awesome power prayer will release in *your* life.